POEMS

Written in Early Youth

P O E M S

Written in Early Youth

BY

T . S . ELIOT

Farrar, Straus and Giroux

NEW YORK

NOTE

These early poems were collected by John Hayward and privately printed in an edition limited to twelve copies by Albert Bonniers of Stockholm in 1950. So much interest has been expressed in this collection, which was supervised by the author, that it seems wise to make it generally available as a corrective to the inaccurate, pirated versions.

These appear to be the only juvenilia of my husband that survive. At the age of nine or ten, he told me, he wrote "a few little verses about the sadness of having to start school again every Monday morning." He gave them to his Mother and hoped they had not been preserved. At about fourteen he wrote "some very gloomy quatrains in the form of the *Rubáiyát*" which had "captured my imagination." These he showed to no one and presumed he destroyed.

Two incidents connected with "A Lyric" (which is given on page 9) remained in the poet's mind. These stanzas in imitation of Ben Jonson were done as a school exercise when he was sixteen. "My English master, who had set his class the task of producing some verse, was much impressed and asked whether I had had any help from some elder person. Surprised, I assured him that they were wholly unaided." They were printed in the school paper, *Smith Academy Record*, but he did not mention them to his family. "Some time later the issue was shown to my Mother, and she remarked (we were walking along Beaumont Street in St. Louis) that she thought them better than anything in verse she had ever written. I knew what her verse meant to her. We did not discuss the matter further."

V. E.

1966

Acknowledgements and thanks are due to the late John Hayward's sister, Mrs. Oakeley, for her permission to reproduce his introduction and notes.

CONTENTS

[*vii*]

INTRODUCTION

Apart from a few unrecorded *jeux d'esprit*, this collection contains all the surviving poems written by T. S. Eliot between the winter of 1904 and the spring of 1910; that is to say, between his sixteenth and twenty-second birthdays, while he was a day-boy at Smith Academy, St. Louis, or an undergraduate at Harvard. *The Death of Saint Narcissus*, which was suppressed in proof and never published, is of a slightly later date.

The first two schoolboy poems were originally published in *Smith Academy Record;* the third was publicly recited by the poet on Graduation Day, 1905, and is here printed for the first time from the only known copy. The nine undergraduate poems, together with a variant version of the "Lyric" printed in *Smith Academy Record*, were originally published between 1907 and 1910 in *The Harvard Advocate*, of which the poet was an associate editor from 1909 to 1910. Eight of these ten poems were reprinted together in *The Harvard Advocate* in 1938; and, without permission, with the addition of the second "Song," in the same periodical in 1948. The ten poems were reissued in the same year by the editors of the *Advocate*, again without permission, and with many misprints, in a pamphlet entitled *The Undergraduate Poems of T. S. Eliot*.

The sources of the text of the present authorized collection are given in the Notes at the end.

JOHN HAYWARD

[*ix*]

POEMS

Written in Early Youth

A Fable for Feasters

In England, long before that royal Mormon
  King Henry VIII found out that monks were quacks,
And took their lands and money from the poor men,
  And brought their abbeys tumbling at their backs,
There was a village founded by some Norman
  Who levied on all travelers his tax;
    Nearby this hamlet was a monastery
    Inhabited by a band of friars merry.

They were possessors of rich lands and wide,
  An orchard, and a vineyard, and a dairy;
Whenever some old villainous baron died,
  He added to their hoards—a deed which ne'er he
Had done before—their fortune multiplied,
  As if they had been kept by a kind fairy.
    Alas! no fairy visited their host,
    Oh, no; much worse than that, they had a ghost.

Some wicked and heretical old sinner
    Perhaps, who had been walled up for his crimes;
At any rate, he sometimes came to dinner,
    Whene'er the monks were having merry times.
He stole the fatter cows and left the thinner
    To furnish all the milk—upset the chimes,
        And once he sat the prior on the steeple,
        To the astonishment of all the people.

When Christmas time was near the Abbot vowed
    They'd eat their meal from ghosts and phantoms free,
The fiend must stay home—no ghosts allowed
    At this exclusive feast. From over sea
He purchased at his own expense a crowd
    Of relics from a Spanish saint—said he:
        'If ghosts come uninvited, then, of course,
        I'll be compelled to keep them off by force.'

He drencht the gown he wore with holy water,
   The turkeys, capons, boars, they were to eat,
He even soakt the uncomplaining porter
   Who stood outside the door from head to feet.
To make a rather lengthy story shorter,
    He left no wise precaution incomplete;
      He doused the room in which they were to dine,
      And watered everything except the wine.

So when all preparations had been made,
   The jovial epicures sat down to table.
The menus of that time I am afraid
   I don't know much about—as well's I'm able
I'll go through the account: They made a raid
   On every bird and beast in Æsop's fable
      To fill out their repast, and pies and puddings,
      And jellies, pasties, cakes among the good things.

A mighty peacock standing on both legs
   With difficulty kept from toppling over,
Next came a viand made of turtle eggs,
   And after that a great pie made of plover,
And flagons which perhaps held several kegs
   Of ale, and cheese which they kept under cover.
      Last, a boar's head, which to bring in took four pages,
      His mouth an apple held, his skull held sausages.

Over their Christmas wassail the monks dozed,
   A fine old drink, though now gone out of use—
His feet upon the table superposed
   Each wisht he had not eaten so much goose.
The Abbot with proposing every toast
   Had drank more than he ought t' have of grape juice.
      The lights began to burn distinctly blue,
      As in ghost stories lights most always do.

The doors, though barred and bolted most securely,
  Gave way—my statement nobody can doubt,
Who knows the well known fact, as you do surely—
  That ghosts are fellows whom you *can't* keep out;
It is a thing to be lamented sorely
  Such slippery folk should be allowed about,
    For often they drop in at awkward moments,
    As everybody'll know who reads this romance.

The Abbot sat as pasted to his chair,
  His eye became the size of any dollar,
The ghost then took him roughly by the hair
  And bade him come with him, in accents hollow.
The friars could do nought but gape and stare,
  The spirit pulled him rudely by the collar,
    And before any one could say 'O jiminy!'
    The pair had vanisht swiftly up the chimney.

Naturally every one searcht everywhere,
  But not a shred of Bishop could be found,
The monks, when anyone questioned, would declare
  St. Peter'd snatcht to heaven their lord renowned,
Though the wicked said (such rascals are not rare)
    That the Abbot's course lay nearer underground;
      But the church straightway put to his name the handle
      Of Saint, thereby rebuking all such scandal.

But after this the monks grew most devout,
  And lived on milk and breakfast food entirely;
Each morn from four to five one took a knout
  And flogged his mates 'till they grew good and friarly.
Spirits from that time forth they did without,
  And lived the admiration of the shire. We
    Got the veracious record of these doings
    From an old manuscript found in the ruins.

[*A Lyric*]

If Time and Space, as Sages say,
    Are things which cannot be,
The sun which does not feel decay
    No greater is than we.
So why, Love, should we ever pray
    To live a century?
The butterfly that lives a day
    Has lived eternity.

The flowers I gave thee when the dew
    Was trembling on the vine,
Were withered ere the wild bee flew
    To suck the eglantine.
So let us haste to pluck anew
    Nor mourn to see them pine,
And though our days of love be few
    Yet let them be divine.

Song

If space and time, as sages say,
    Are things that cannot be,
The fly that lives a single day
    Has lived as long as we.
But let us live while yet we may,
    While love and life are free,
For time is time, and runs away,
    Though sages disagree.

The flowers I sent thee when the dew
    Was trembling on the vine
Were withered ere the wild bee flew
    To suck the eglantine.
But let us haste to pluck anew
    Nor mourn to see them pine,
And though the flowers of life be few
    Yet let them be divine.

[*At Graduation 1905*]

I

Standing upon the shore of all we know
We linger for a moment doubtfully,
Then with a song upon our lips, sail we
Across the harbor bar—no chart to show,
No light to warn of rocks which lie below,
But let us yet put forth courageously.

II

As colonists embarking from the strand
To seek their fortunes on some foreign shore
Well know they lose what time shall not restore,
And when they leave they fully understand
That though again they see their fatherland
They there shall be as citizens no more.

III

We go; as lightning-winged clouds that fly
After a summer tempest, when some haste
North, South, and Eastward o'er the water's waste,
Some to the western limits of the sky
Which the sun stains with many a splendid dye,
Until their passing may no more be traced.

IV

Although the path be tortuous and slow,
Although it bristle with a thousand fears,
To hopeful eye of youth it still appears
A lane by which the rose and hawthorn grow.
We hope it may be; would that we might know!
Would we might look into the future years.

V

Great duties call—the twentieth century
More grandly dowered than those which came before,
Summons—who knows what time may hold in store,
Or what great deeds the distant years may see,
What conquest over pain and misery,
What heroes greater than were e'er of yore!

V I

But if this century is to be more great
Than those before, her sons must make her so,
And we are of her sons, and we must go
With eager hearts to help mold well her fate,
And see that she shall gain such proud estate
As shall on future centuries bestow

VII

A legacy of benefits—may we
In future years be found with those who try
To labor for the good until they die,
And ask no other guerdon than to know
That they have helpt the cause to victory,
That with their aid the flag is raised on high.

VIII

Sometime in distant years when we are grown
Gray-haired and old, whatever be our lot,
We shall desire to see again the spot
Which, whatsoever we have been or done
Or to what distant lands we may have gone,
Through all the years will ne'er have been forgot.

IX

For in the sanctuaries of the soul
Incense of altar-smoke shall rise to thee
From spotless fanes of lucid purity,
O school of ours! The passing years that roll
Between, as we press onward to the goal,
Shall not have power to quench the memory.

X

We shall return; and it will be to find
A different school from that which now we know;
But only in appearance 'twill be so.
That which has made it great, not left behind,
The same school in the future shall we find
As this from which as pupils now we go.

XI

We go; like flitting faces in a dream;
Out of thy care and tutelage we pass
Into the unknown world—class after class,
O queen of schools—a momentary gleam,
A bubble on the surface of the stream,
A drop of dew upon the morning grass;

XII

Thou dost not die—for each succeeding year
Thy honor and thy fame shall but increase
Forever, and may stronger words than these
Proclaim thy glory so that all may hear;
May worthier sons be thine, from far and near
To spread thy name o'er distant lands and seas!

XIII

As thou to thy departing sons hast been
To those that follow may'st thou be no less;
A guide to warn them, and a friend to bless
Before they leave thy care for lands unseen;
And let thy motto be, proud and serene,
Still as the years pass by, the word "Progress!"

XIV

So we are done; we may no more delay;
Thus is the end of every tale: "Farewell,"
A word that echoes like a funeral bell
And one that we are ever loth to say.
But 'tis a call we cannot disobey,
Exeunt omnes, with a last "farewell."

Song

When we came home across the hill
  No leaves were fallen from the trees;
  The gentle fingers of the breeze
Had torn no quivering cobweb down.

The hedgerow bloomed with flowers still,
  No withered petals lay beneath;
  But the wild roses in your wreath
Were faded, and the leaves were brown.

Before Morning

While all the East was weaving red with gray,
The flowers at the window turned toward dawn,
Petal on petal, waiting for the day,
Fresh flowers, withered flowers, flowers of dawn.

This morning's flowers and flowers of yesterday
Their fragrance drifts across the room at dawn,
Fragrance of bloom and fragrance of decay,
Fresh flowers, withered flowers, flowers of dawn.

Circe's Palace

Around her fountain which flows
With the voice of men in pain,
Are flowers that no man knows.
Their petals are fanged and red
With hideous streak and stain;
They sprang from the limbs of the dead.—
We shall not come here again.

Panthers rise from their lairs
In the forest which thickens below,
Along the garden stairs
The sluggish python lies;
The peacocks walk, stately and slow,
And they look at us with the eyes
Of men whom we knew long ago.

On a Portrait

Among a crowd of tenuous dreams, unknown
To us of restless brain and weary feet,
Forever hurrying, up and down the street,
She stands at evening in the room alone.

Not like a tranquil goddess carved of stone
But evanescent, as if one should meet
A pensive lamia in some wood-retreat,
An immaterial fancy of one's own.

No meditations glad or ominous
Disturb her lips, or move the slender hands;
Her dark eyes keep their secrets hid from us,
Beyond the circle of our thought she stands.

The parrot on his bar, a silent spy,
Regards her with a patient curious eye.

Song

The moonflower opens to the moth,
The mist crawls in from sea;
A great white bird, a snowy owl,
Slips from the alder tree.

Whiter the flowers, Love, you hold,
Than the white mist on the sea;
Have you no brighter tropic flowers
With scarlet life, for me?

Nocturne

Romeo, *grand sérieux*, to importune
Guitar and hat in hand, beside the gate
With Juliet, in the usual debate
Of love, beneath a bored but courteous moon;
The conversation failing, strikes some tune
Banal, and out of pity for their fate
Behind the wall I have some servant wait,
Stab, and the lady sinks into a swoon.

Blood looks effective on the moonlit ground—
The hero smiles; in my best mode oblique
Rolls toward the moon a frenzied eye profound,
(No need of "Love forever?"—"Love next week?")
While female readers all in tears are drowned:—
"The perfect climax all true lovers seek!"

Humouresque

(AFTER J. LAFORGUE)

One of my marionettes is dead,
Though not yet tired of the game—
But weak in body as in head,
(A jumping-jack has such a frame).

But this deceaséd marionette
I rather liked: a common face,
(The kind of face that we forget)
Pinched in a comic, dull grimace;

Half bullying, half imploring air,
Mouth twisted to the latest tune;
His who-the-devil-are-you stare;
Translated, maybe, to the moon.

With Limbo's other useless things
Haranguing spectres, set him there;
"The snappiest fashion since last spring's,
"The newest style, on Earth, I swear.

"Why don't you people get some class?
(Feebly contemptuous of nose),
"Your damned thin moonlight, worse than gas—
"Now in New York"—and so it goes.

Logic a marionette's, all wrong
Of premises; yet in some star
A hero!—Where would he belong?
But, even at that, what mask *bizarre!*

Spleen

Sunday: this satisfied procession
Of definite Sunday faces;
Bonnets, silk hats, and conscious graces
In repetition that displaces
Your mental self-possession
By this unwarranted digression.

Evening, lights, and tea!
Children and cats in the alley;
Dejection unable to rally
Against this dull conspiracy.

And Life, a little bald and gray,
Languid, fastidious, and bland,
Waits, hat and gloves in hand,
Punctilious of tie and suit
(Somewhat impatient of delay)
    On the doorstep of the Absolute.

Ode

THOMAS STEARNS ELIOT

For the hour that is left us Fair Harvard, with thee,
    Ere we face the importunate years,
In thy shadow we wait, while thy presence dispels
    Our vain hesitations and fears.
And we turn as thy sons ever turn, in the strength
    Of the hopes that thy blessings bestow,
From the hopes and ambitions that sprang at thy feet
    To the thoughts of the past as we go.

Yet for all of these years that to-morrow has lost
    We are still the less able to grieve,
With so much that of Harvard we carry away
    In the place of the life that we leave.
And only the years that efface and destroy
    Give us also the vision to see
What we owe for the future, the present, and past,
    Fair Harvard, to thine and to thee.

The Death of Saint Narcissus

Come under the shadow of this gray rock—
Come in under the shadow of this gray rock,
And I will show you something different from either
Your shadow sprawling over the sand at daybreak, or
Your shadow leaping behind the fire against the red rock:
I will show you his bloody cloth and limbs
And the gray shadow on his lips.

He walked once between the sea and the high cliffs
When the wind made him aware of his limbs smoothly
        passing each other
And of his arms crossed over his breast.
When he walked over the meadows
He was stifled and soothed by his own rhythm.
By the river
His eyes were aware of the pointed corners of his eyes
And his hands aware of the pointed tips of his fingers.

Struck down by such knowledge
He could not live men's ways, but became a dancer before
    God
If he walked in city streets
He seemed to tread on faces, convulsive thighs and knees.
So he came out under the rock.

First he was sure that he had been a tree,
Twisting its branches among each other
And tangling its roots among each other.

Then he knew that he had been a fish
With slippery white belly held tight in his own fingers,
Writhing in his own clutch, his ancient beauty
Caught fast in the pink tips of his new beauty.

Then he had been a young girl
Caught in the woods by a drunken old man
Knowing at the end the taste of his own whiteness
The horror of his own smoothness,
And he felt drunken and old.

So he became a dancer to God.
Because his flesh was in love with the burning arrows
He danced on the hot sand
Until the arrows came.
As he embraced them his white skin surrendered itself to the
    redness of blood, and satisfied him.
Now he is green, dry and stained
With the shadow in his mouth.

NOTES

NOTES

Page 3

A FABLE FOR FEASTERS

Text from the original version in *Smith Academy Record*, Vol. 8. No. 2, February 1905. Signed: "T. E. '05." The original text has the following misprints:

l. 29 a crowd] at crowd
l. 32 to keep] to to keep
l. 84 snatcht] snacht

This Byronic exercise was Eliot's first appearance in print.

Page 9

[A LYRIC:] *"If Time and Space, as Sages say"*

Printed from the original holograph manuscript in the possession of King's College, Cambridge (John Hayward Bequest). This, the earliest surviving poetical MS. by T. S. Eliot is written in ink on one side of a quarto sheet of ruled paper, and subscribed at the foot of the page: "(Doggerel License No. 3,271,574)." There is no title. The verso is superscribed: "Eliot | January 24th 1905." Below in red ink is the credit mark "A" in the hand of the English master at Smith Academy — "a certain Mr. Roger Conant Hatch [who] conceived great hopes of a literary career for me." (T. S. E. to J. H. August 19th, 1943.) First printed, with the title "A Lyric," in *Smith Academy Record*, viii, 4, April 1905.

Page 10

SONG: *"If space and time, as sages say"*

The variant version of "A Lyric" as printed in *The Harvard Advocate*, lxxxiii, 7, June 3rd, 1907.

Page 11

[AT GRADUATION 1905]

Printed from the only surviving copy, an untitled and unsigned typescript in the possession of King's College, Cambridge (John Haywood Bequest). Written a few months after the preceding poem, and recited by the poet on Graduation Day at Smith Academy, 1905. "I hope you will be impressed by the pathos of the hopes which I expressed for the twentieth century and for the future of a day school which was dissolved through lack of pupils a few years later." (T. S. E. to J. H. August 19th, 1943.) The text of the typescript copy has been emended in the following places:
    l. 36 bestow] bestow.
    l. 44 lot,] lot
    l. 53 goal,] goal
    l. 62 thy] they
    l. 84 "farewell".] "farewell."

Page 18

SONG: *"When we came home across the hill"*

Text from the original version in *The Harvard Advocate*, lxxxiii, 6, May 24th, 1907. Signed: "T. S. Eliot."
    l. 5 still,] still.

Notes

Page 19

BEFORE MORNING

Text from the original version in *The Harvard Advocate*, lxxxvi, 4, November 13th, 1908. Signed: "T. S. E."

Page 20

CIRCE'S PALACE

Text from the original version in *The Harvard Advocate*, lxxxvi, 5, November 25th, 1908. Signed: "T. S. Eliot."

Page 21

ON A PORTRAIT

Text from the original version in *The Harvard Advocate*, lxxxvi, 9, January 26th, 1909. Signed: "T. S. Eliot."
l. 13 spy,] spy.

Page 22

SONG: *"The moonflower opens to the moth"*

Text from the original version in *The Harvard Advocate*, lxxxvi, 9, January 26th, 1909. Signed: "T. S. E." Not included in *The Harvard Advocate* reprints of 1938 and 1948. First reprinted in *The Undergraduate Poems of T. S. Eliot*, 1948.

Page 23

NOCTURNE

Text from the original version in *The Harvard Advocate,* lxxxviii, 3, November 12th, 1909. Signed: "T. S. Eliot."

Page 24

HUMOURESQUE (*after J. Laforgue*)

Text from the original version in *The Harvard Advocate,* lxxxviii, 7, January 12th, 1910. Signed: "T. S. Eliot."
l. 18 nose] hose
l. 24 mask] mark
These two misprints are noted and corrected in ink by the poet in his own copy of *The Harvard Advocate* reprint of 1938. They remain uncorrected in *The Harvard Advocate* reprint of 1948, and in *The Undergraduate Poems of T. S. Eliot,* 1948. The theme of this exercise in the manner of Laforgue was suggested by the second stanza of his "Locutions de Pierrot, xii": —

> Encore un de mes pierrots mort;
> Mort d'un chronique orphelinisme;
> C'était un coeur plein de dandyisme
> Lunaire, en un drôle de corps.

Page 26

SPLEEN

Text from the original version in *The Harvard Advocate,* lxxxviii, 8, January 26th, 1910. Signed: "T. S. Eliot."

Page 27

ODE

Text from the version printed in *The Harvard Advocate*, lxxxix, 8, June 24th, 1910. Not included in *The Harvard Advocate* reprint of 1938. The "Ode" was also published simultaneously in the printed programme of "Harvard Class Day 1910 [Friday, June 24th] Week," with the following variants: —

title: ODE] The ODE. Programme omits signature.

l. 1 us Fair] us, fair

l. 3 wait, while] wait while

l. 5 turn, in] turn in

l. 7 From the hopes] The hopes

l. 8 past as] past, as

l. 9 these years] the years

The "Ode" was reprinted the same day in the *Boston Evening Transcript* and the *Boston Evening Herald*. As "Odist" of the Harvard Class of 1910 T. S. Eliot recited his "Class Ode" in the Sanders Theater at Harvard in the forenoon of Class Day. The "Poet" of the Harvard Class of 1910 was Edward Eyre Hunt of Mechanicsburg, Ohio.

Page 28

THE DEATH OF SAINT NARCISSUS

Text from the unique *Poetry* (Chicago) galley proof, preserved in the Harriet Monroe Collection in the University of Chicago. The proof, which consists of two galleys (15 and 16), is printed on one side of a single slip headed "POEMS." The letterpress, which is broken after the line "If he walked in city streets," is scored through by hand with the manuscript directive "Kill" (i.e., suppress) in the margin of each section. In the top right-hand corner of the proof there is a manuscript editorial note: "Jewel file | This poem | never pub'd | T. S. Eliot." There is no evidence to show when this poem was submitted to *Poetry* (Chicago), of which Harriet Monroe was the founder and editor, or when it was set in type. There was an interval of five years between the Harvard "Class Ode" and Eliot's next appearance in print, with "The Love Song of J. Alfred Prufrock," which was published, on the recommendation of Ezra Pound, in the June 1915 issue of *Poetry* (Chicago), though it had actually been completed in 1911. "The Death of Saint Narcissus" was probably written during this interval, but it was certainly not set in type with a view to publication until after the appearance of "Prufrock." On the other hand, the fact that its opening lines were to be incorporated almost exactly in *The Waste Land* (1922) should not be taken to indicate a later date for its composition. Cf. *The Waste Land* 25–29:

> There is a shadow under this red rock,
> (Come in under the shadow of this red rock).
> And I will show you something different from either
> Your shadow at morning striding behind you
> Or your shadow at evening rising to meet you . . .